EASY Flowers COLORING BOOK

COLOR TEST PAGE

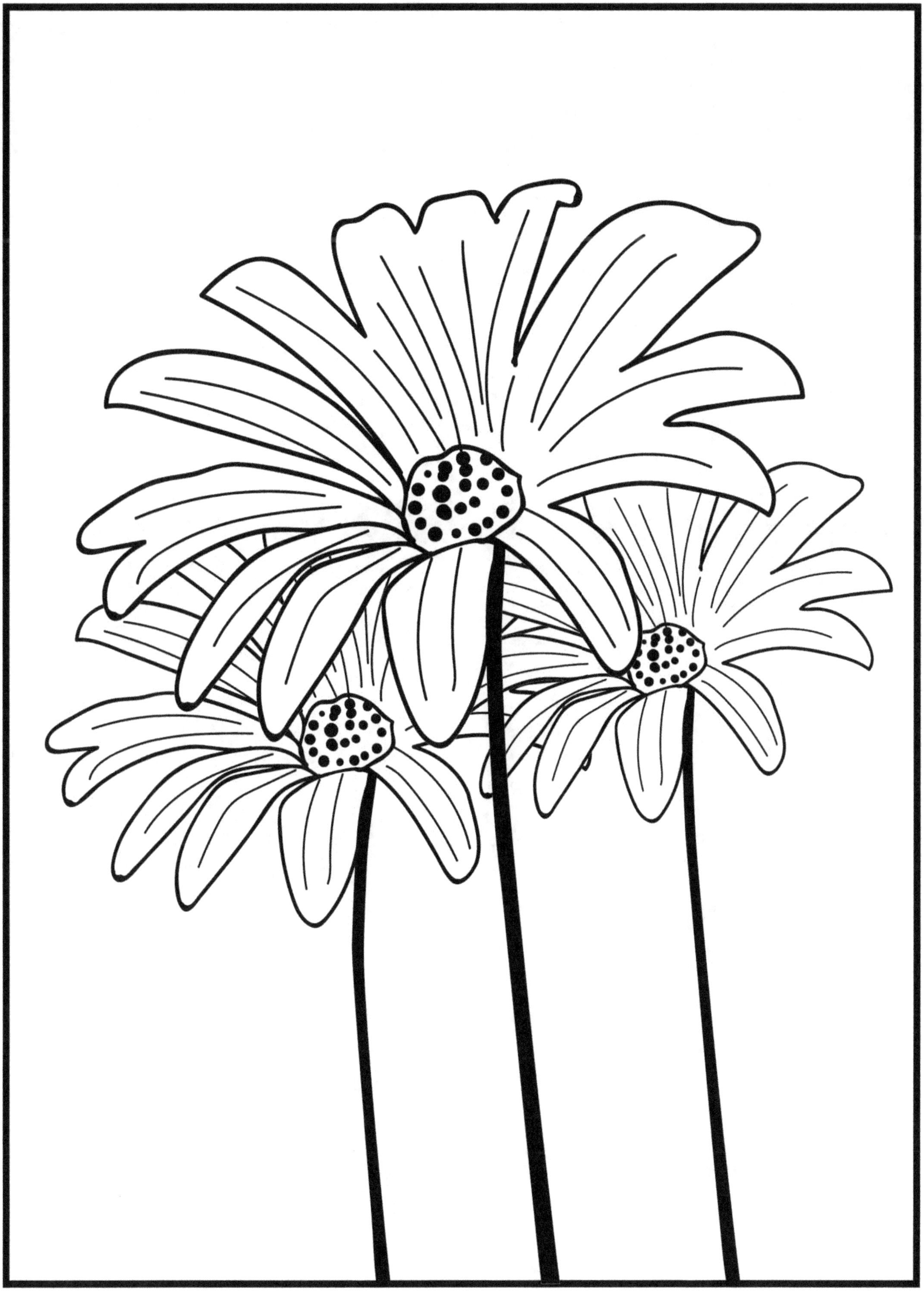

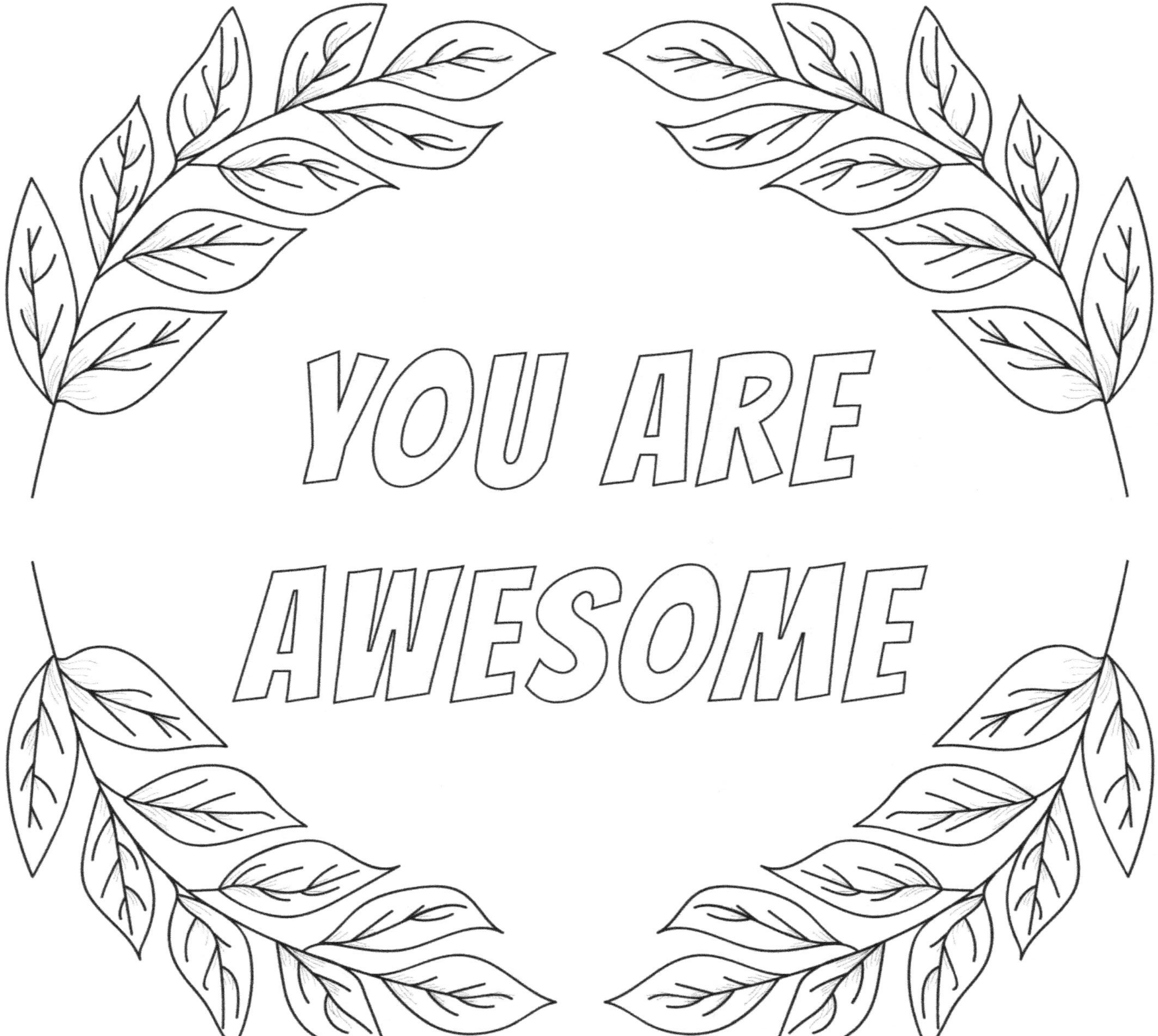
YOU ARE
AWESOME

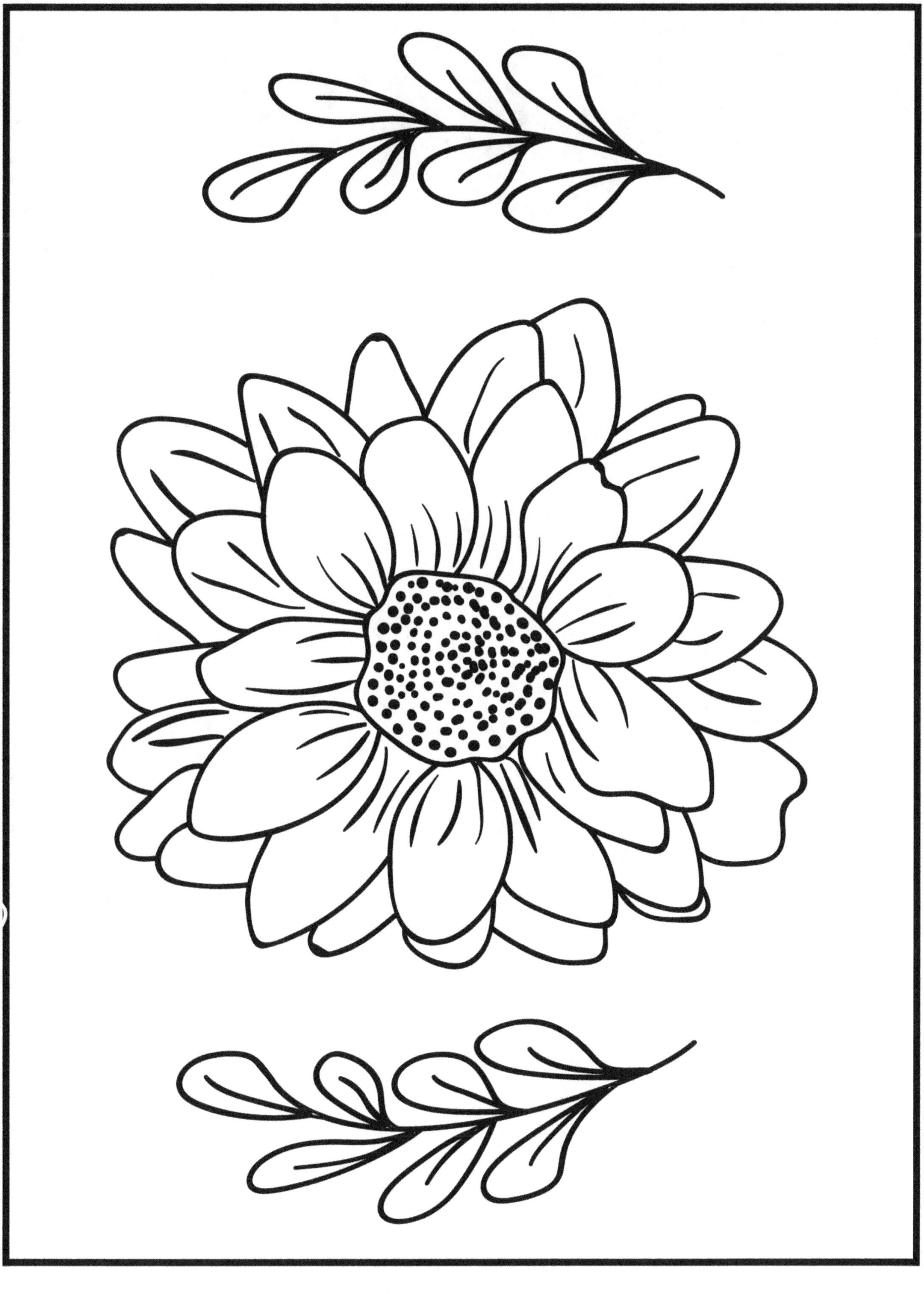

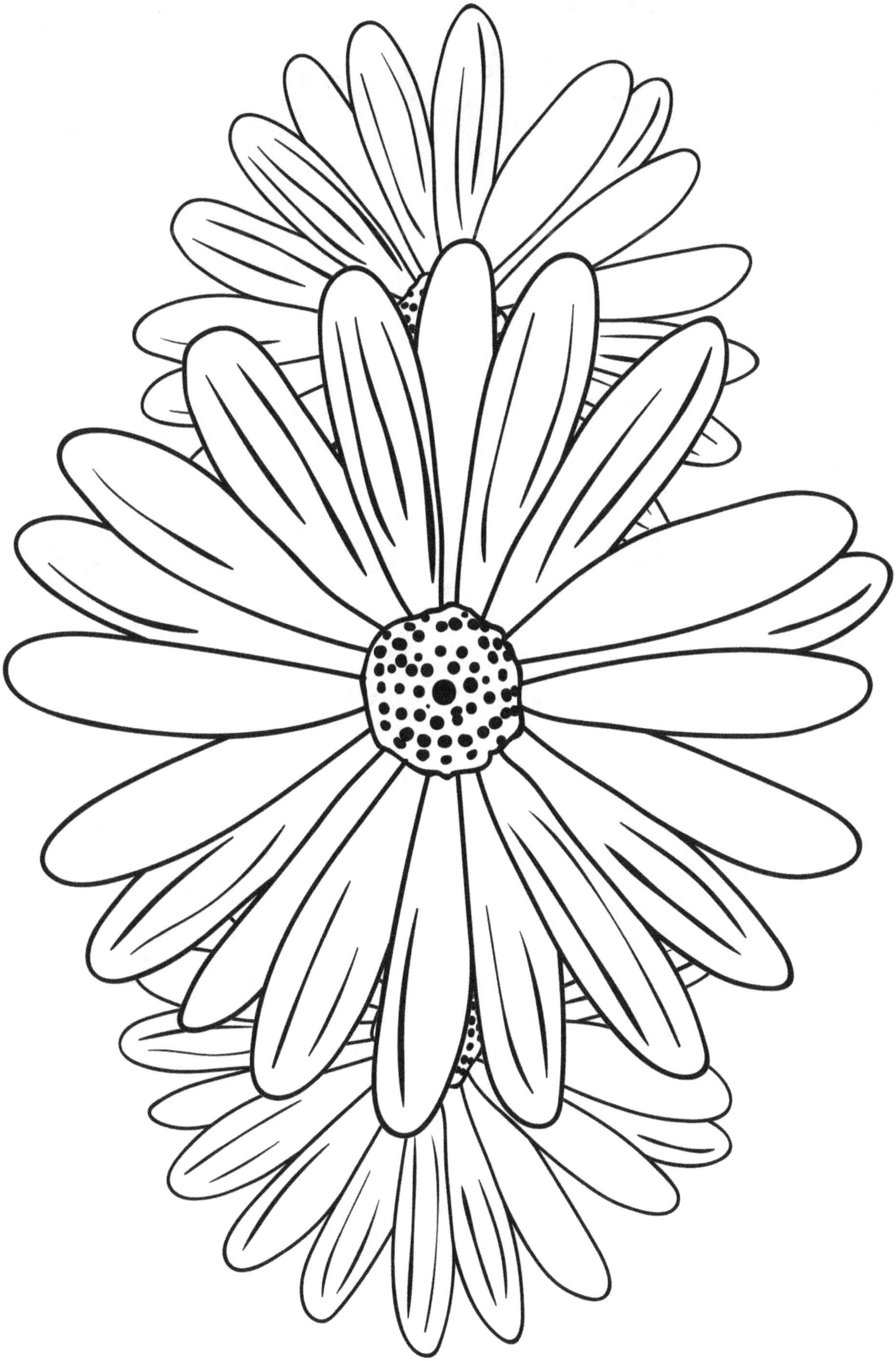

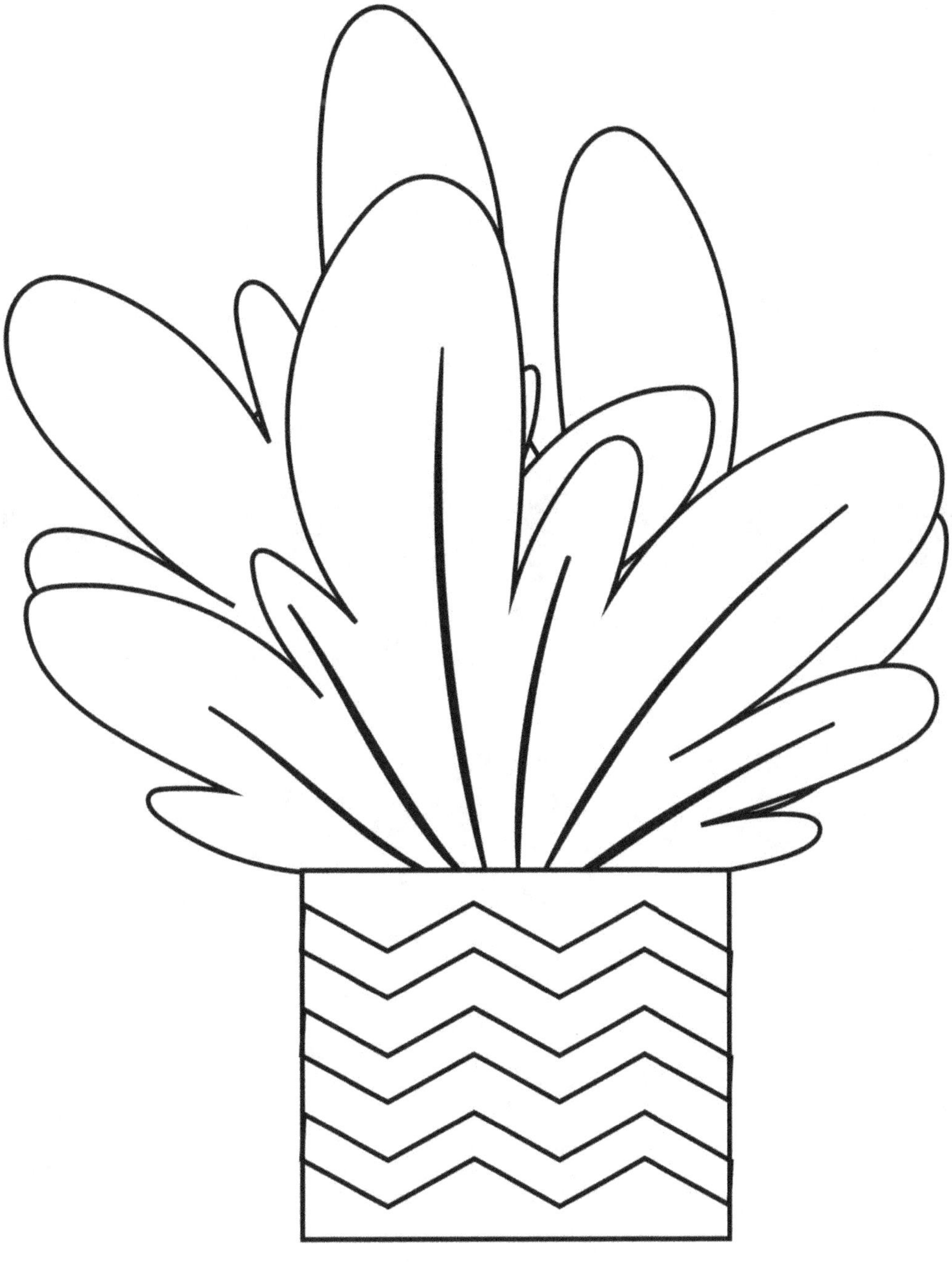

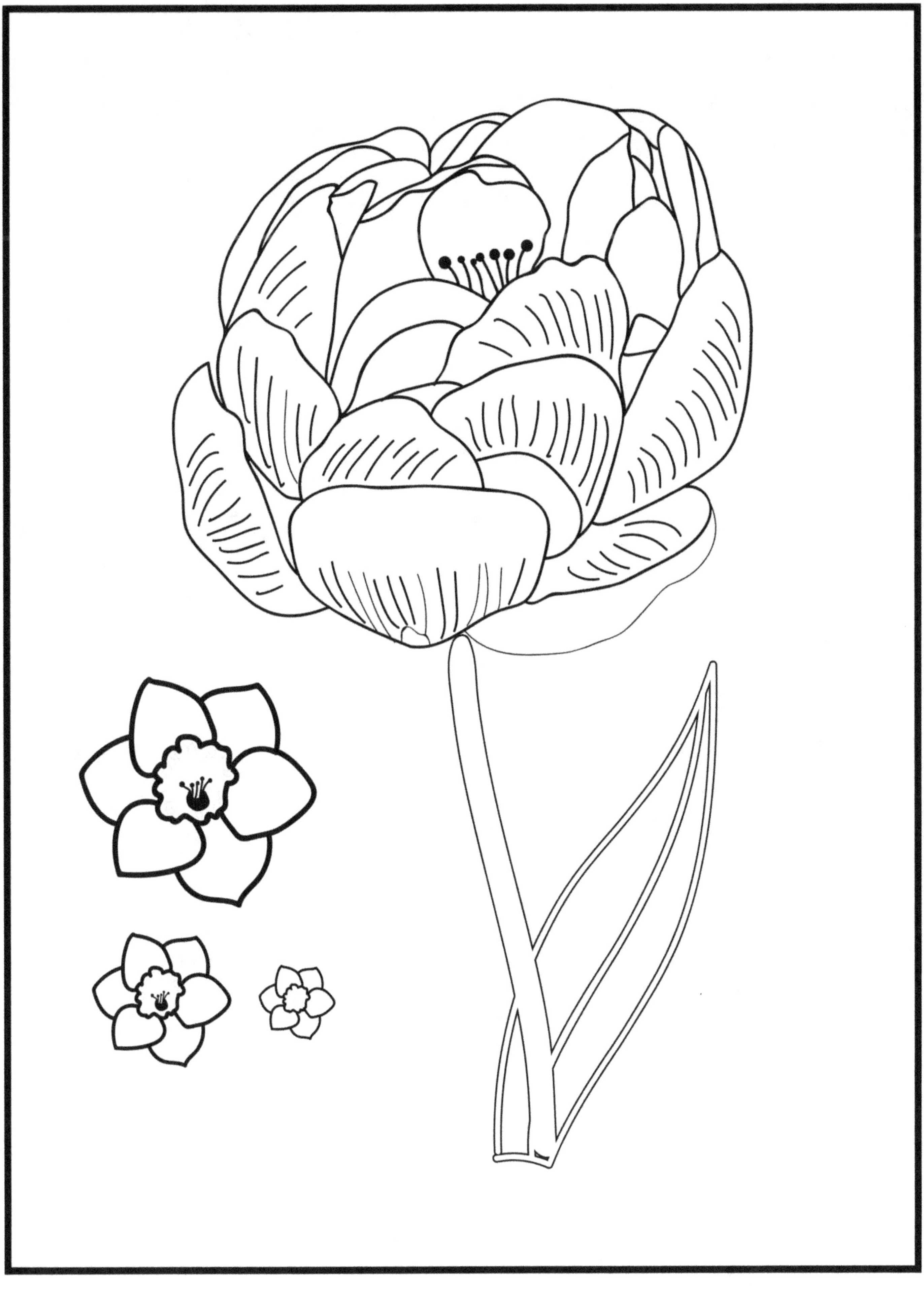

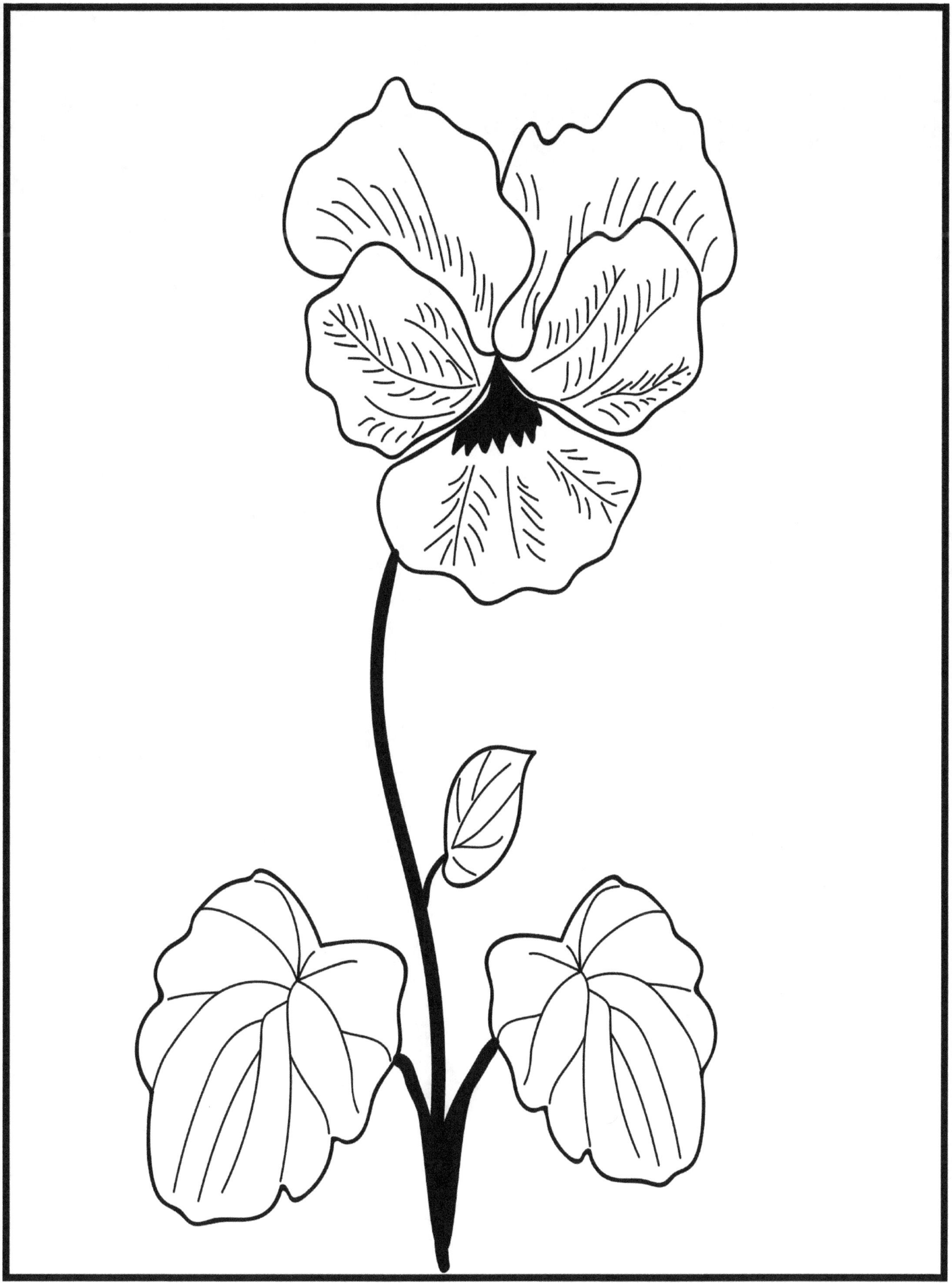

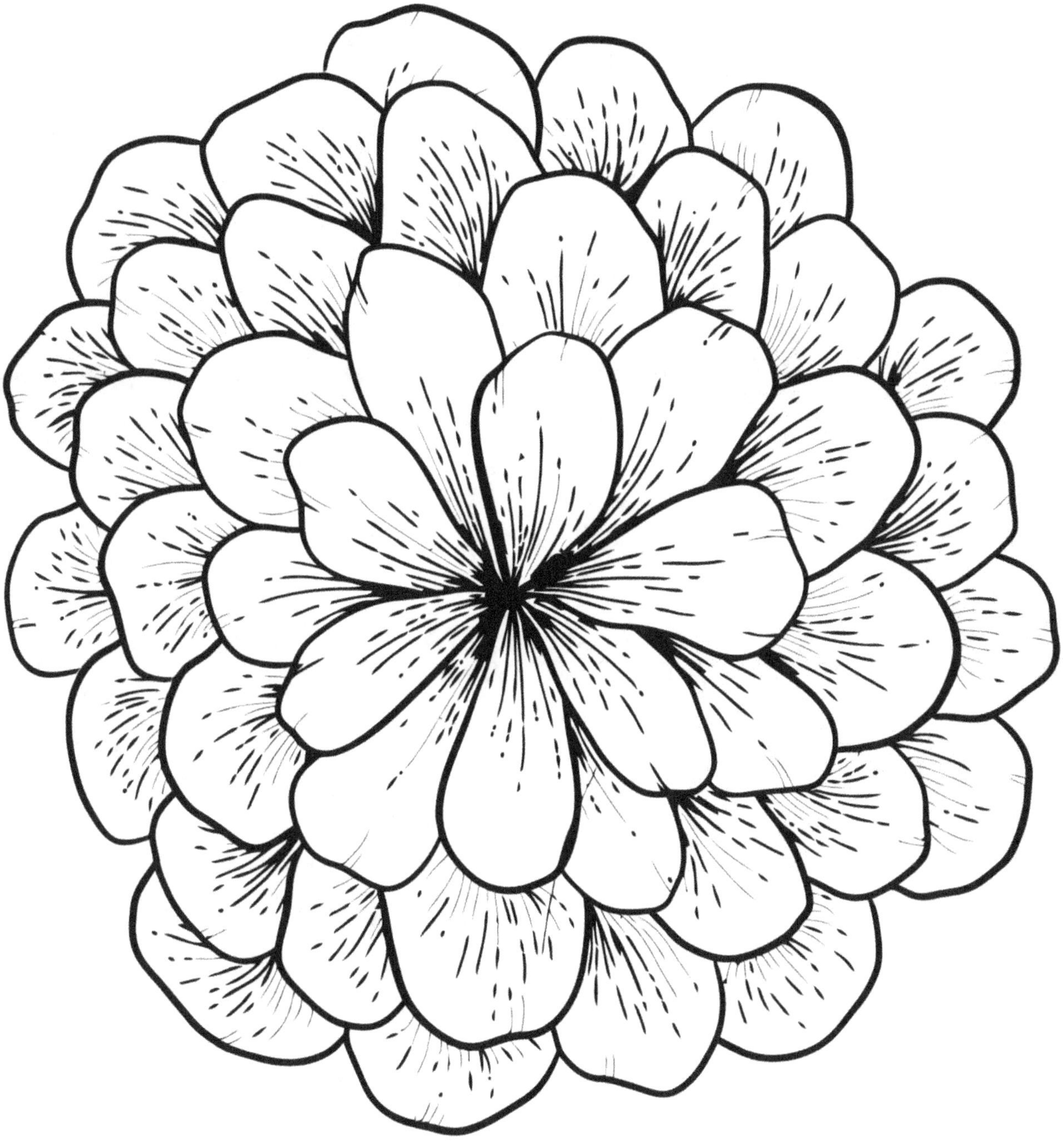

Today is a Good Day

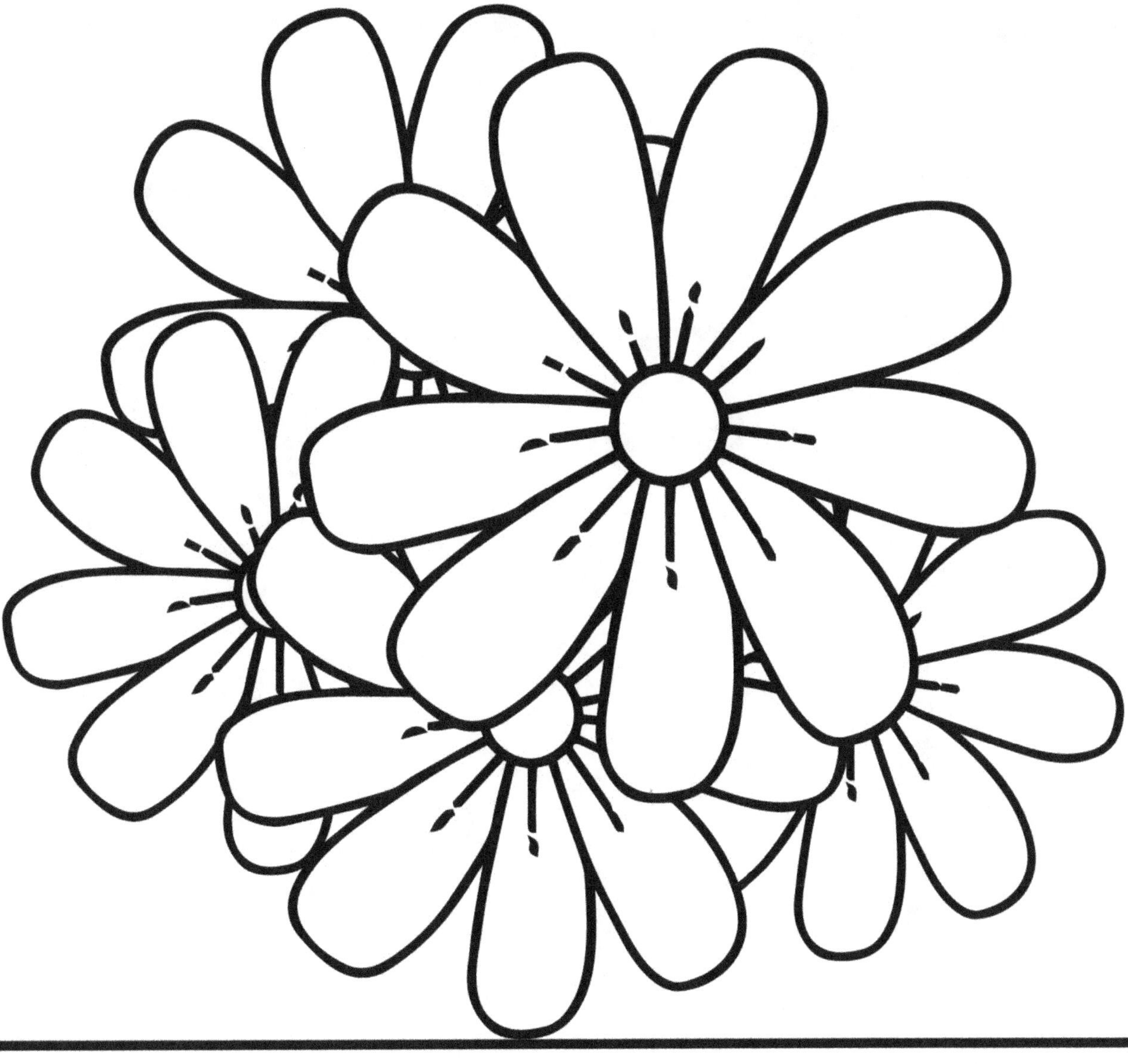

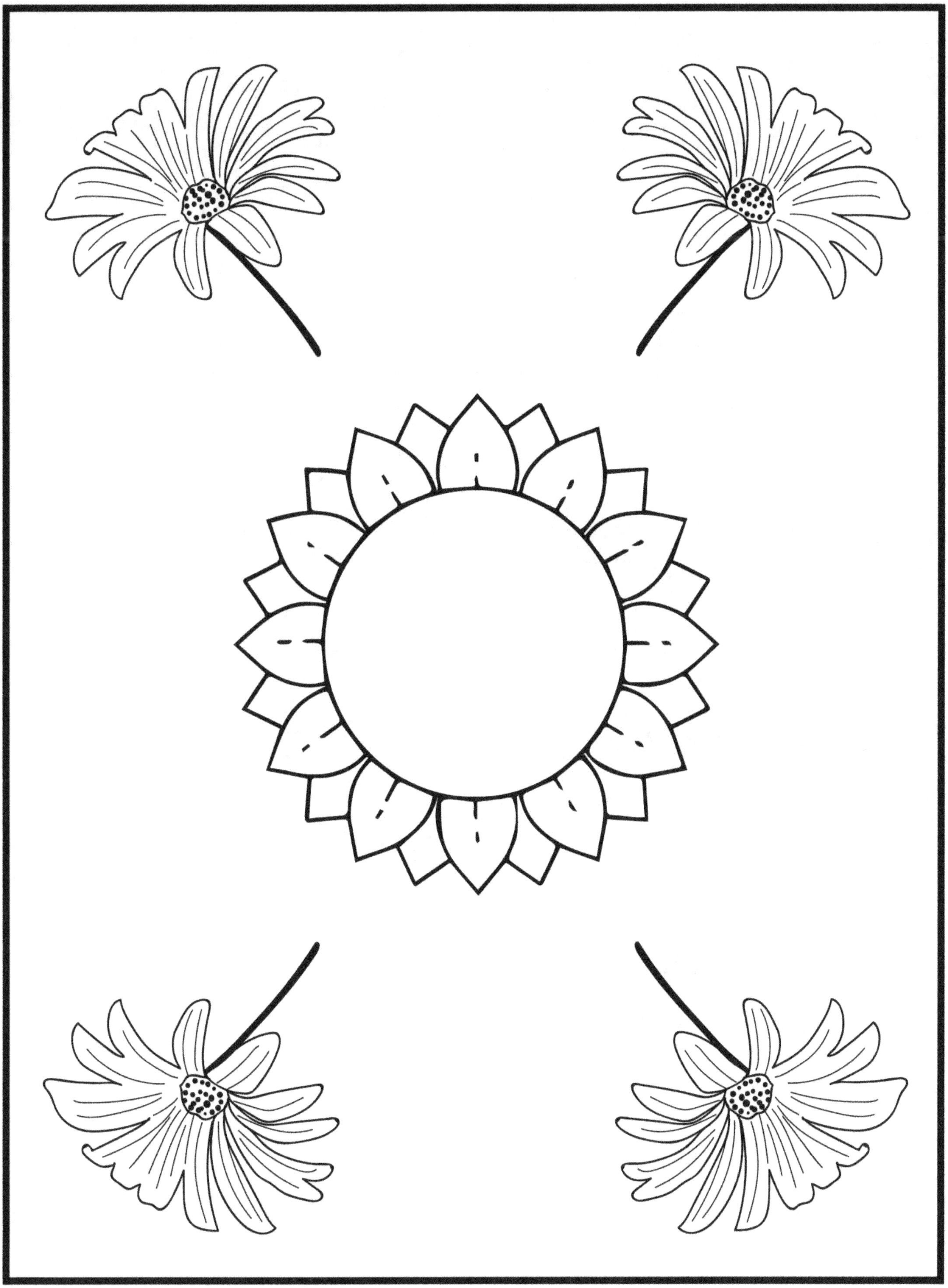

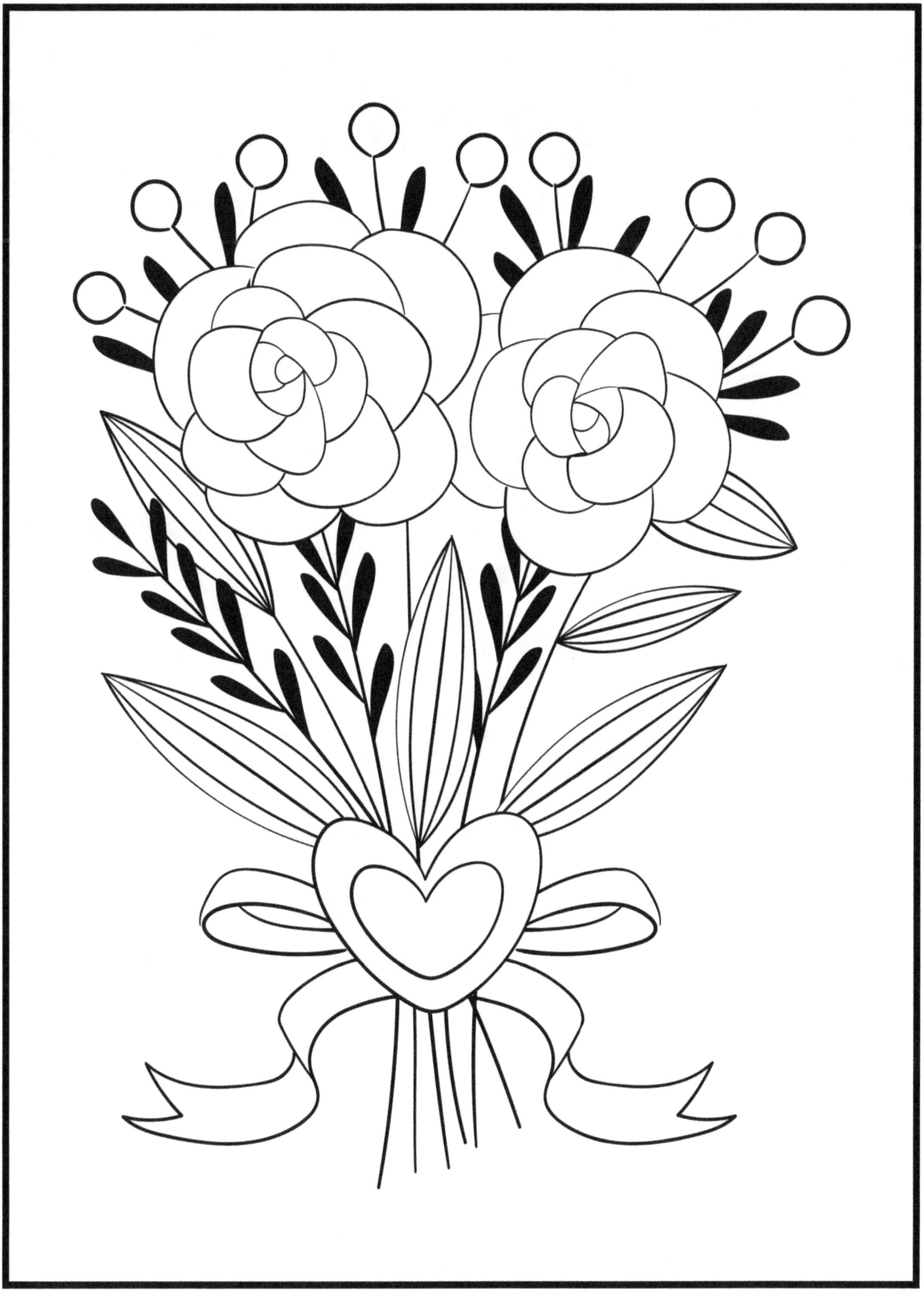

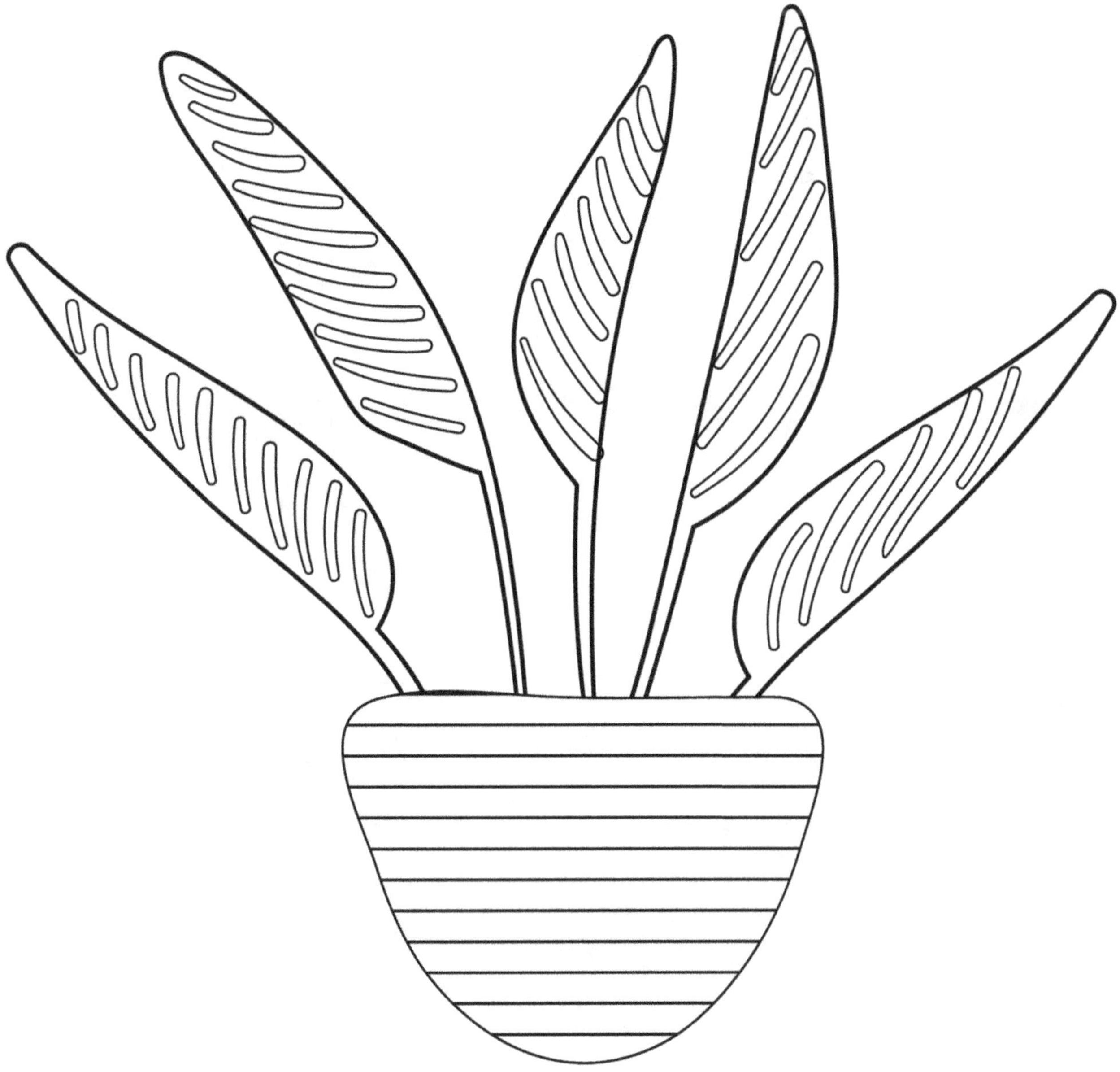

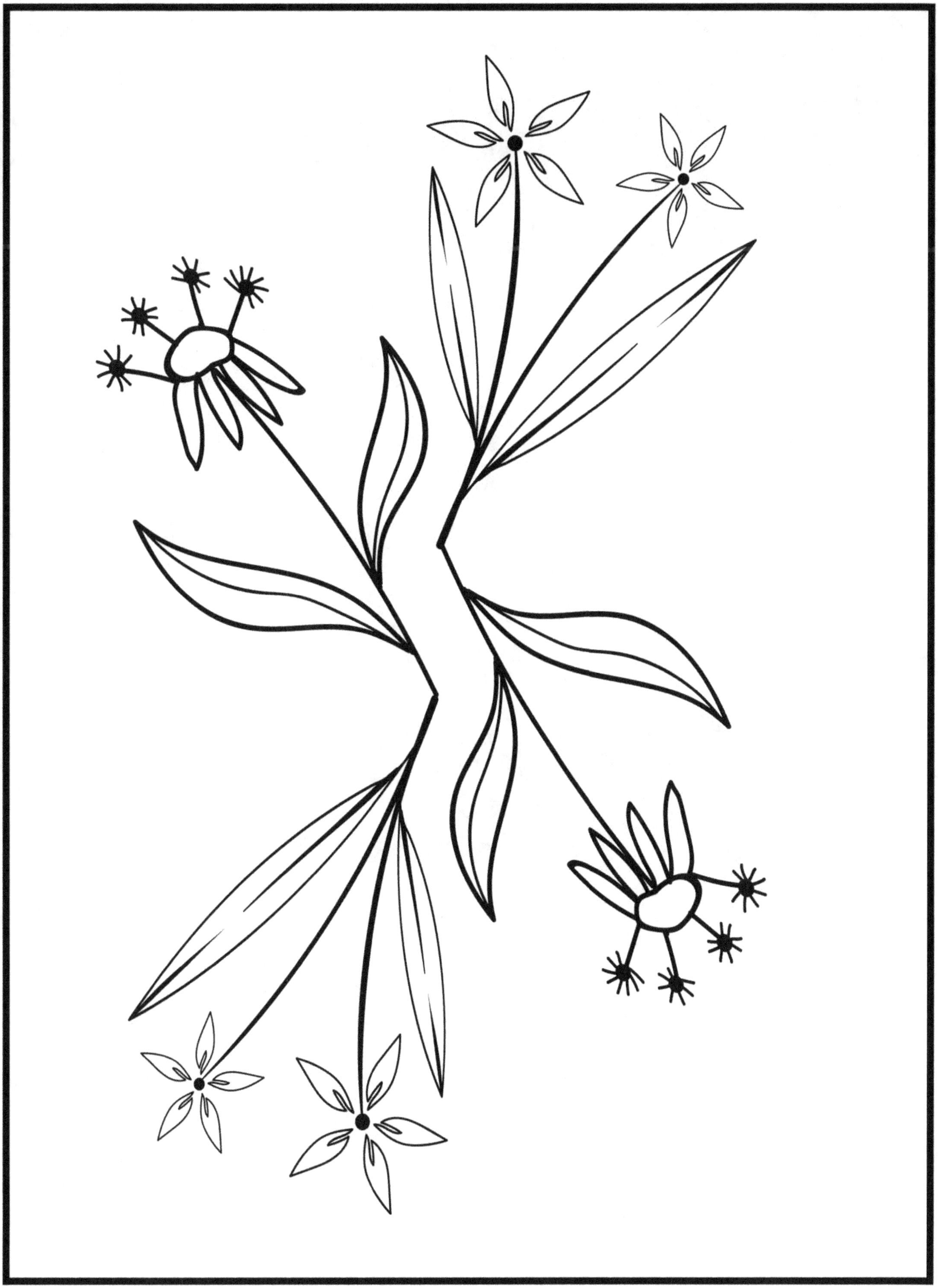

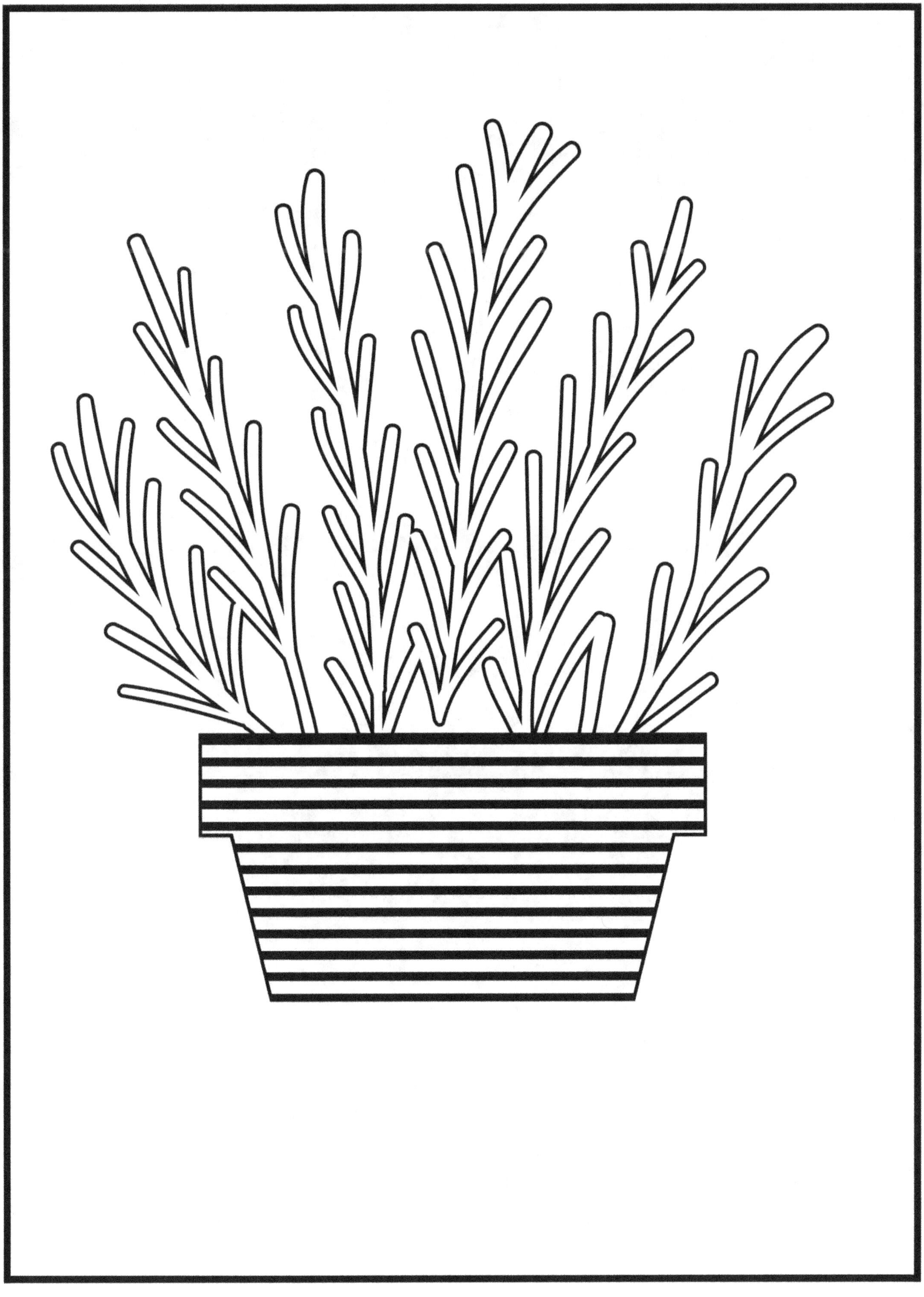

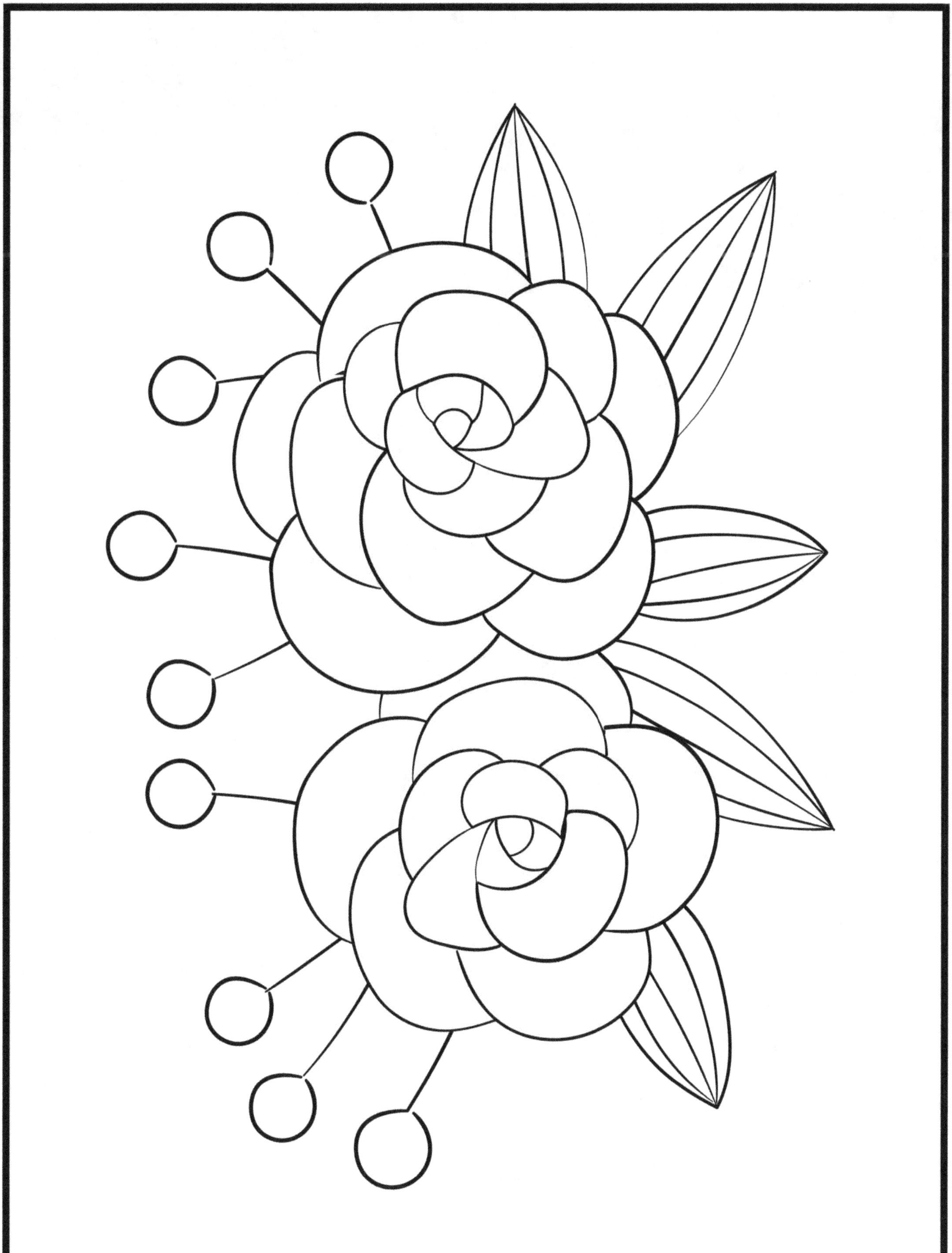

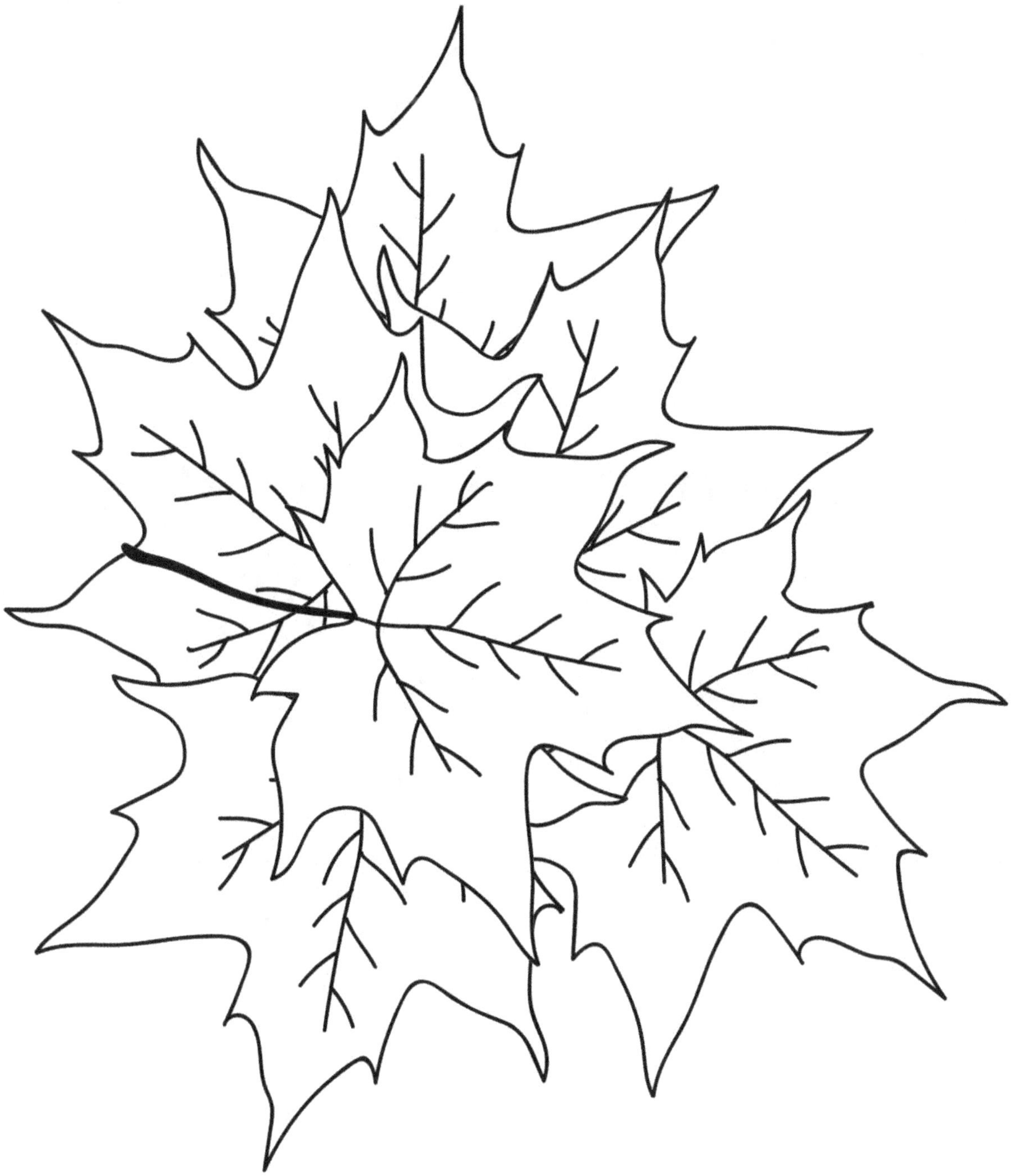

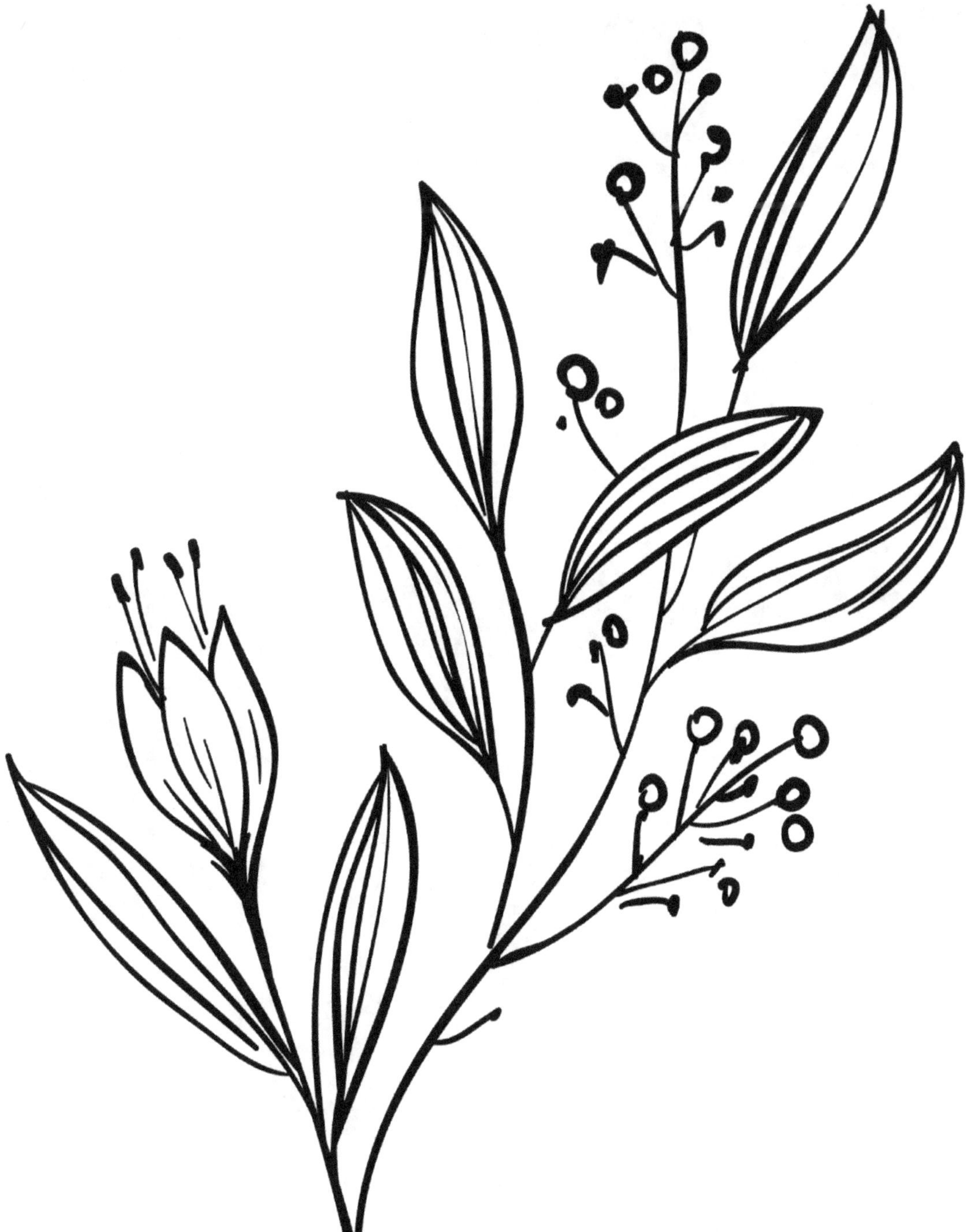

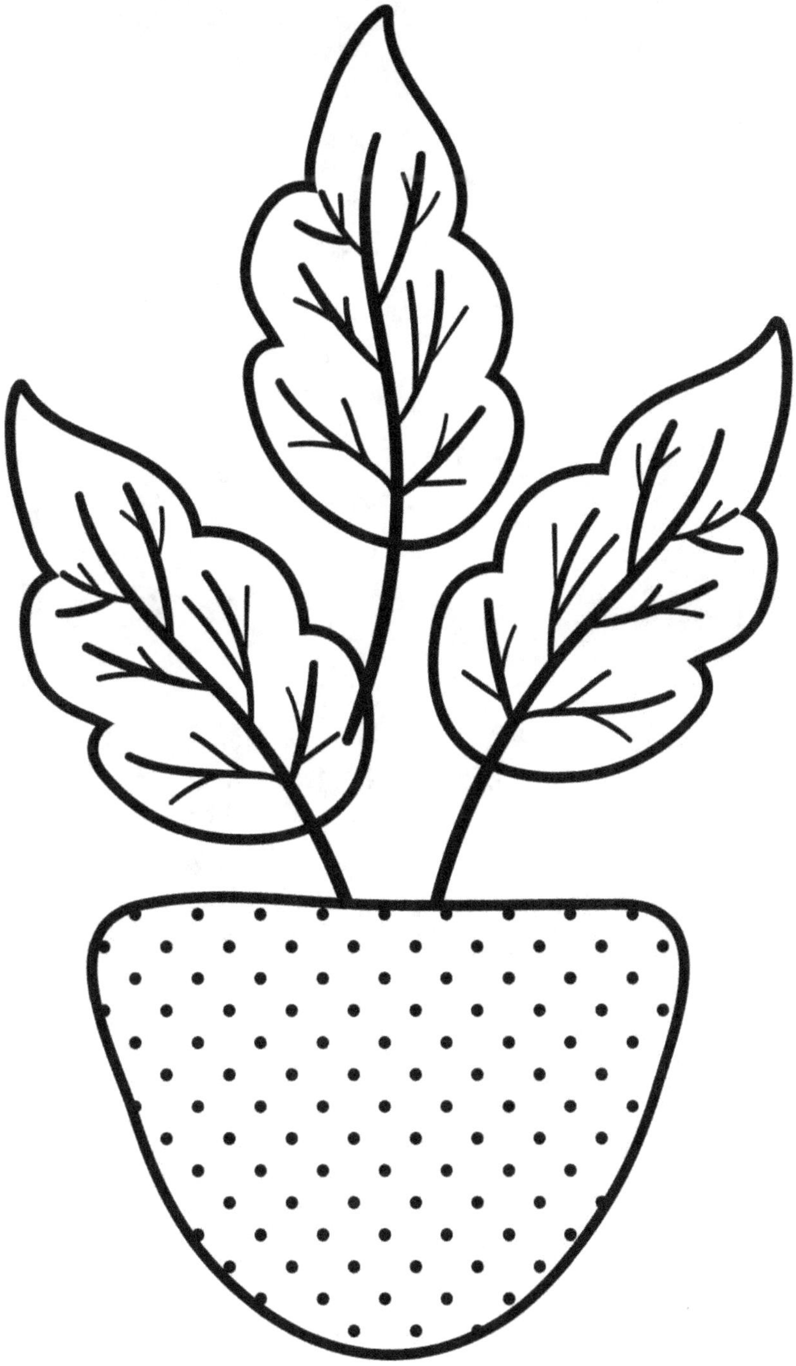

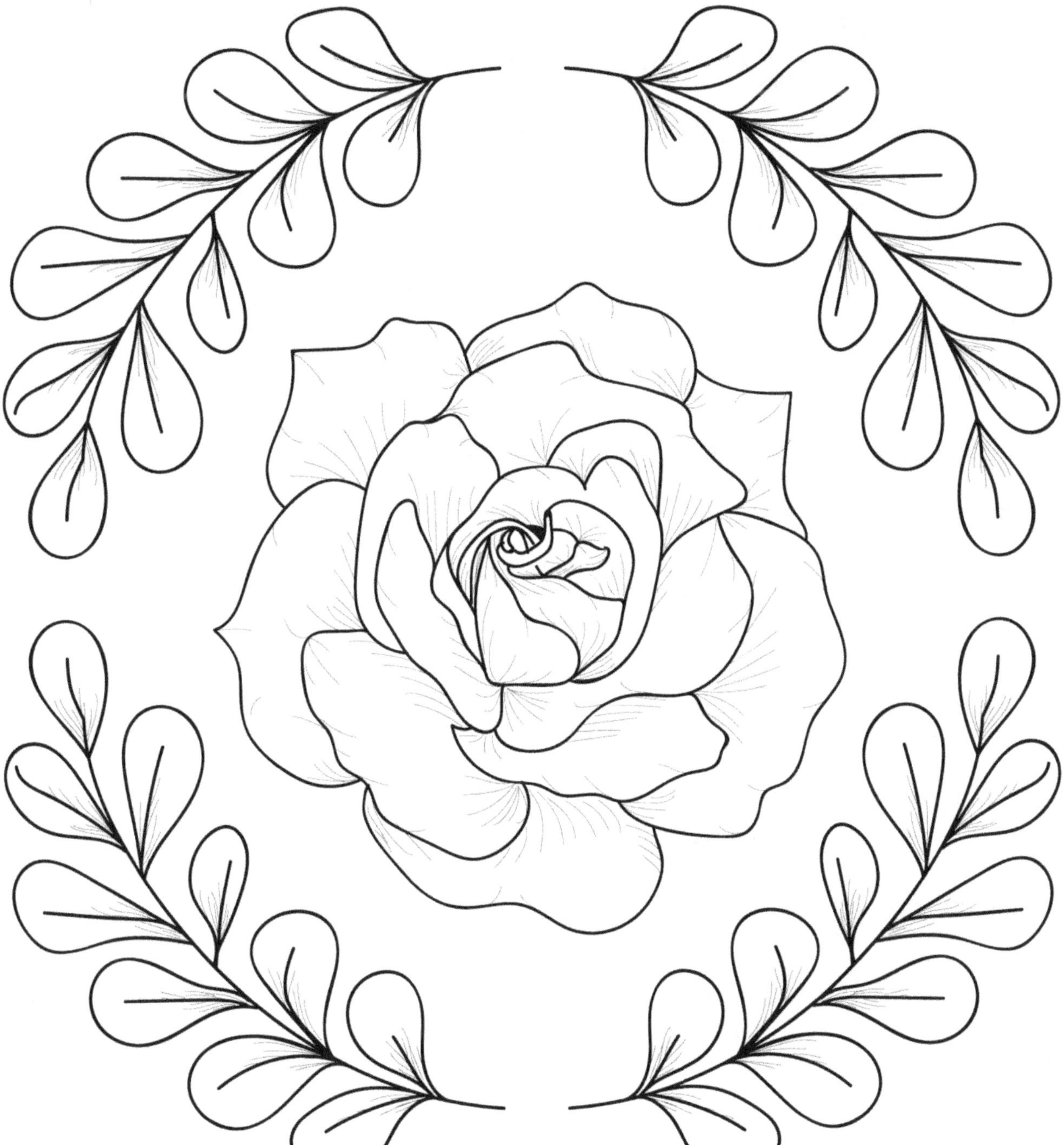

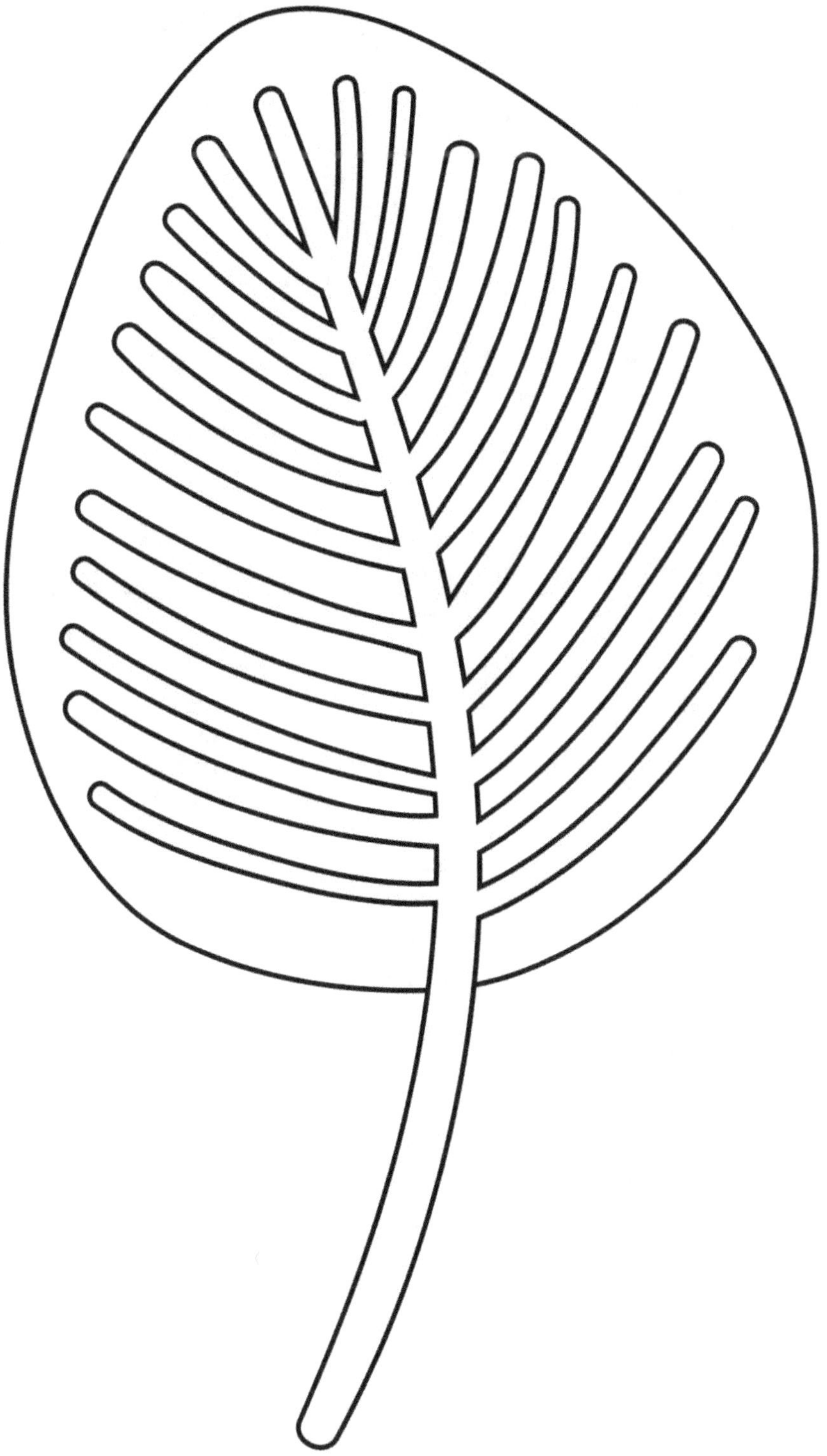

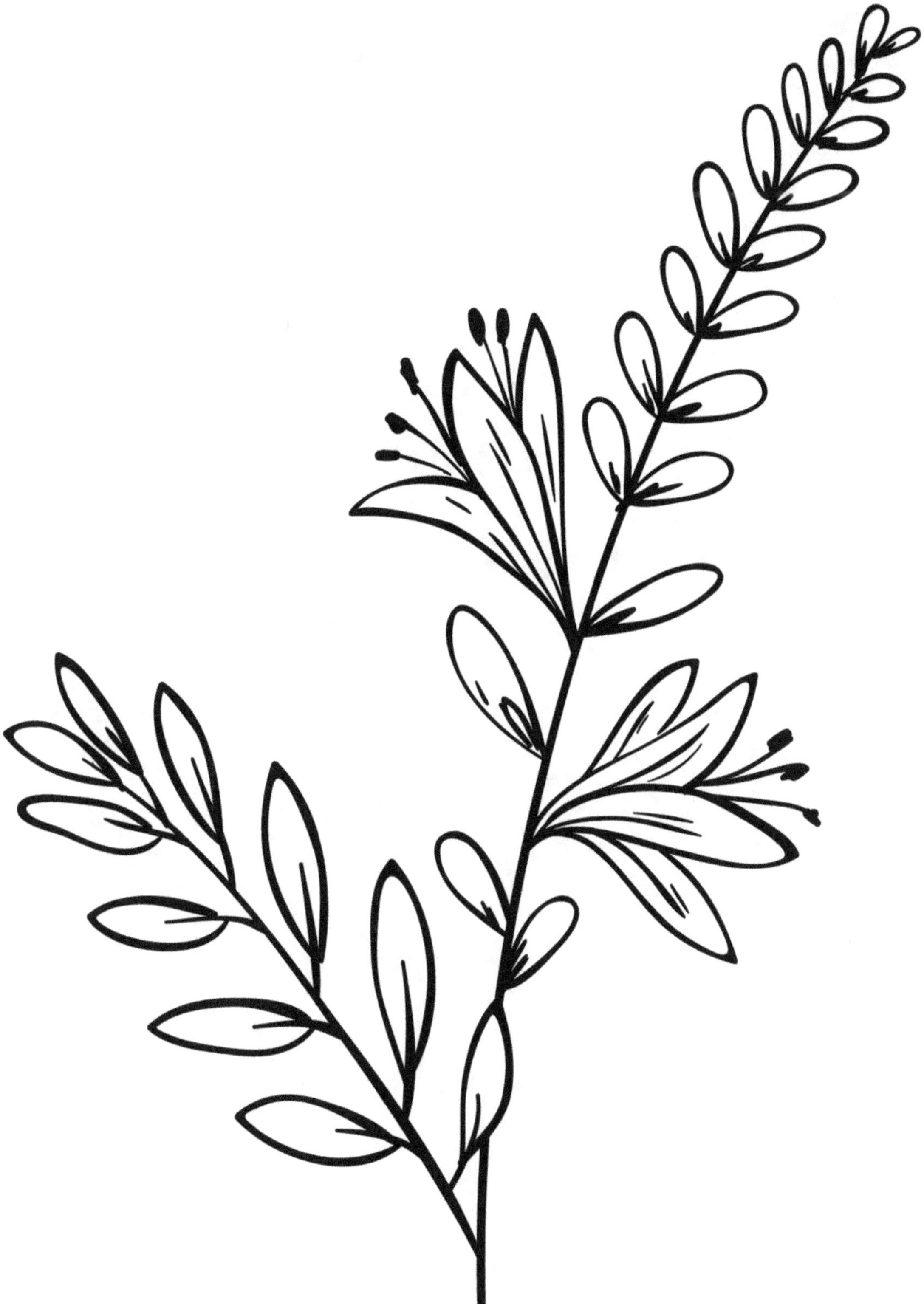

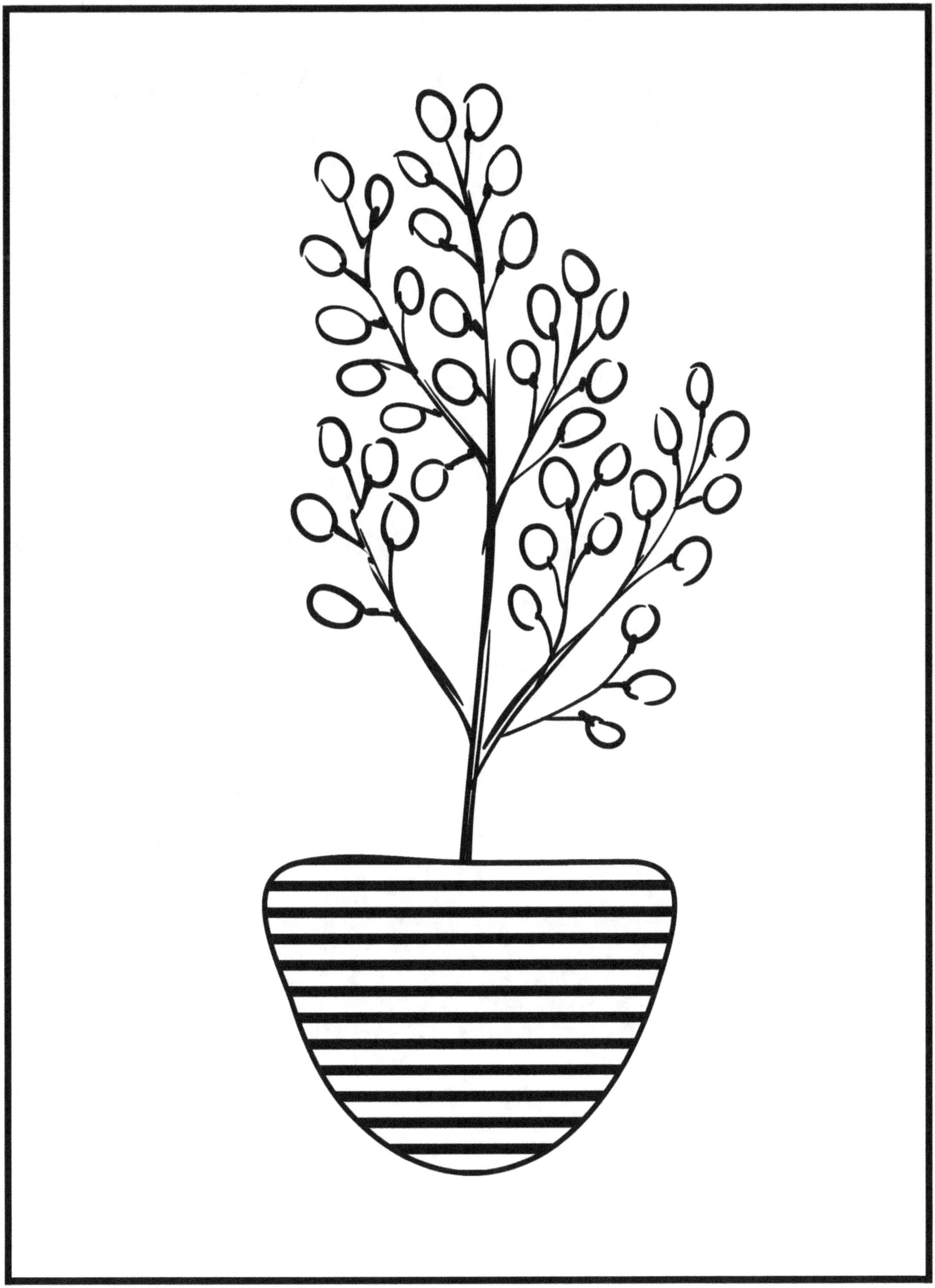

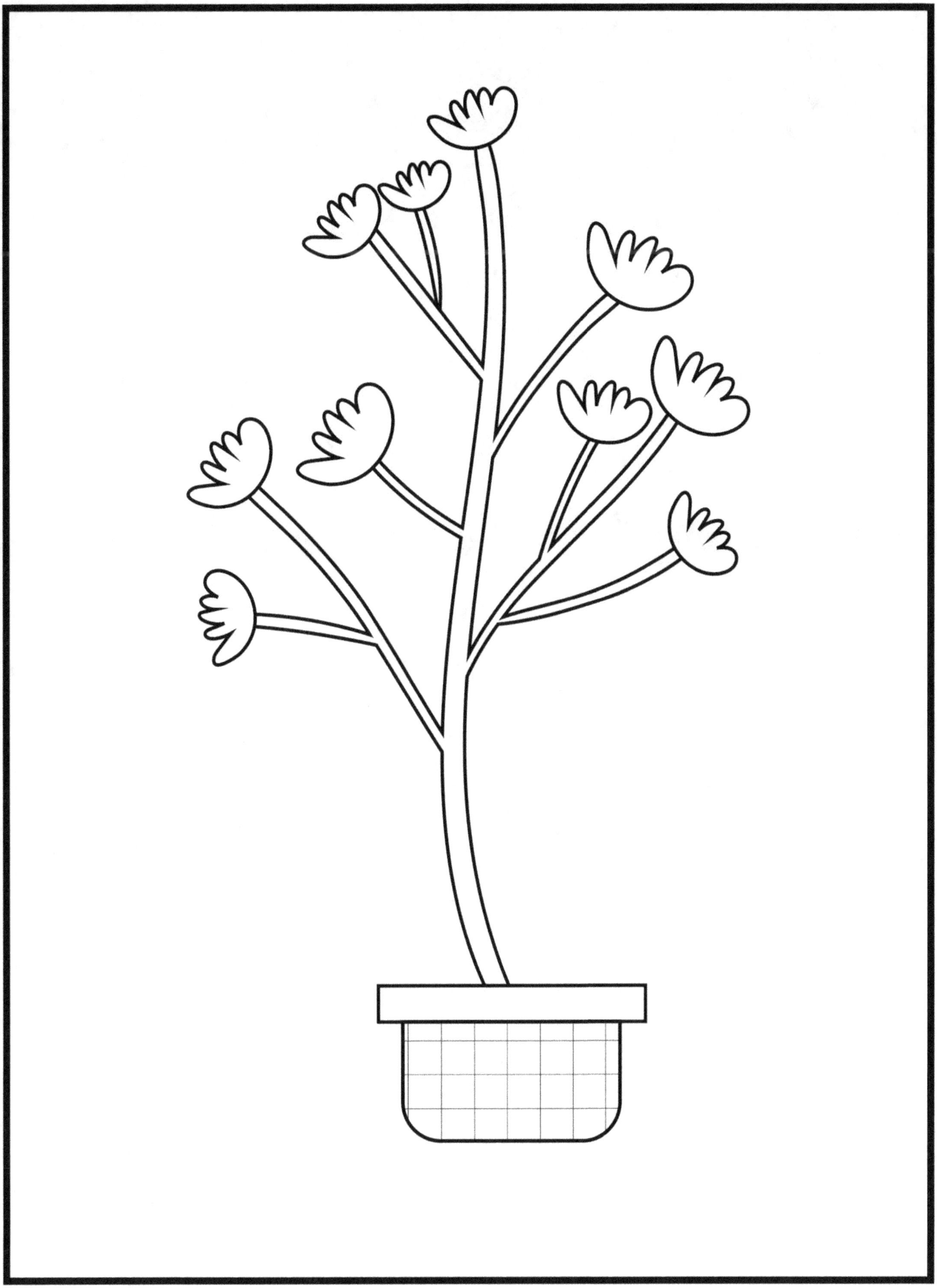

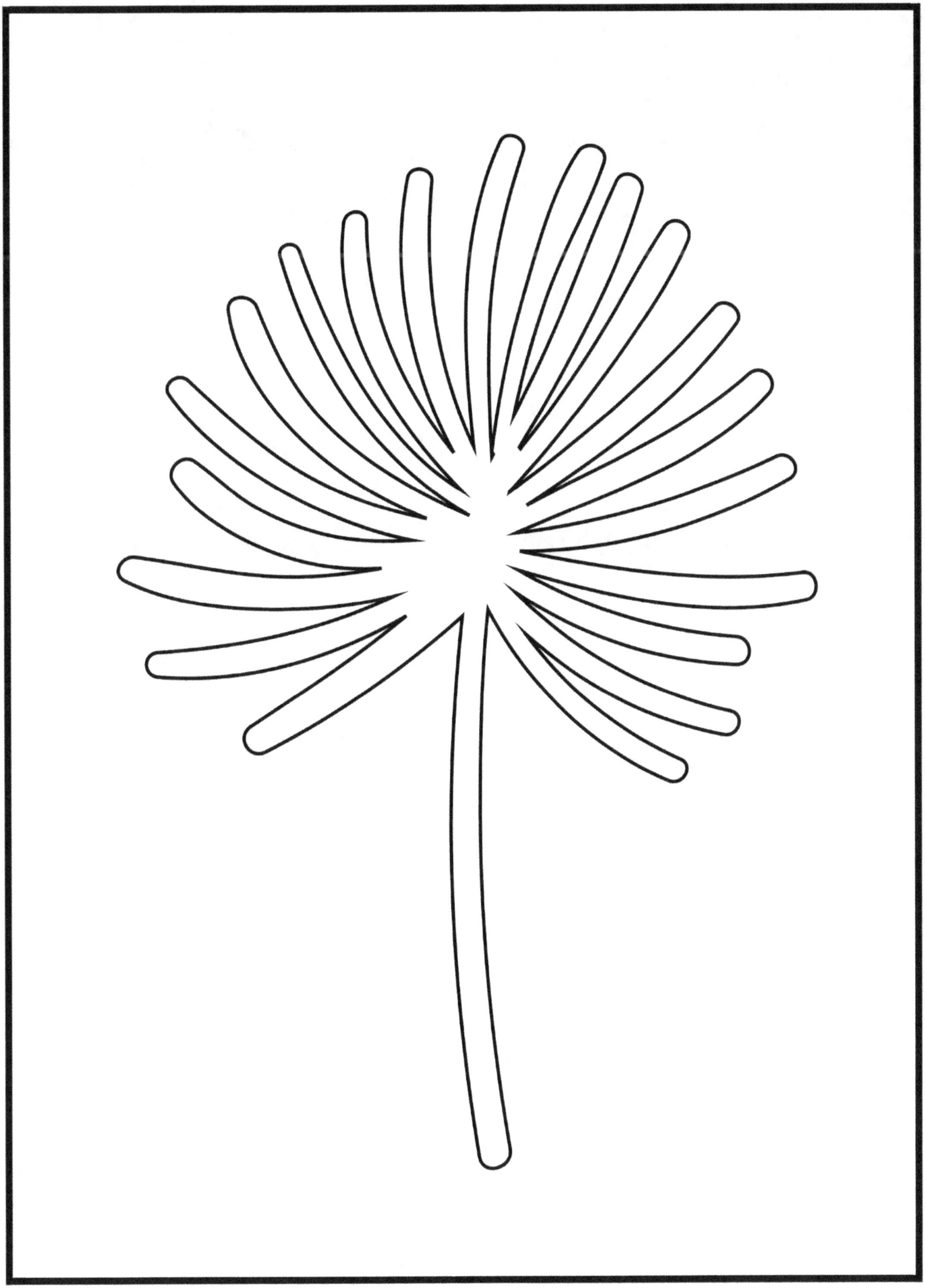

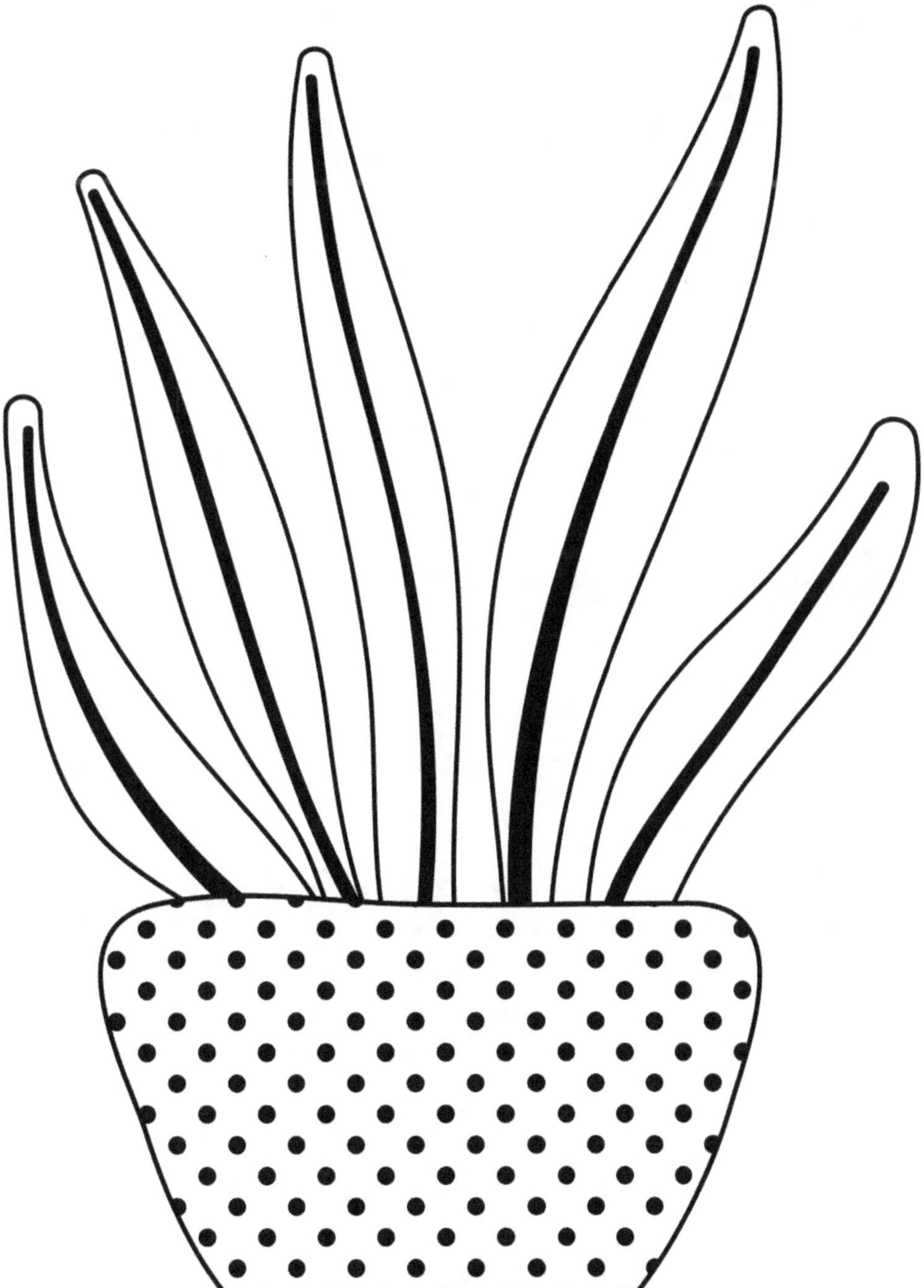

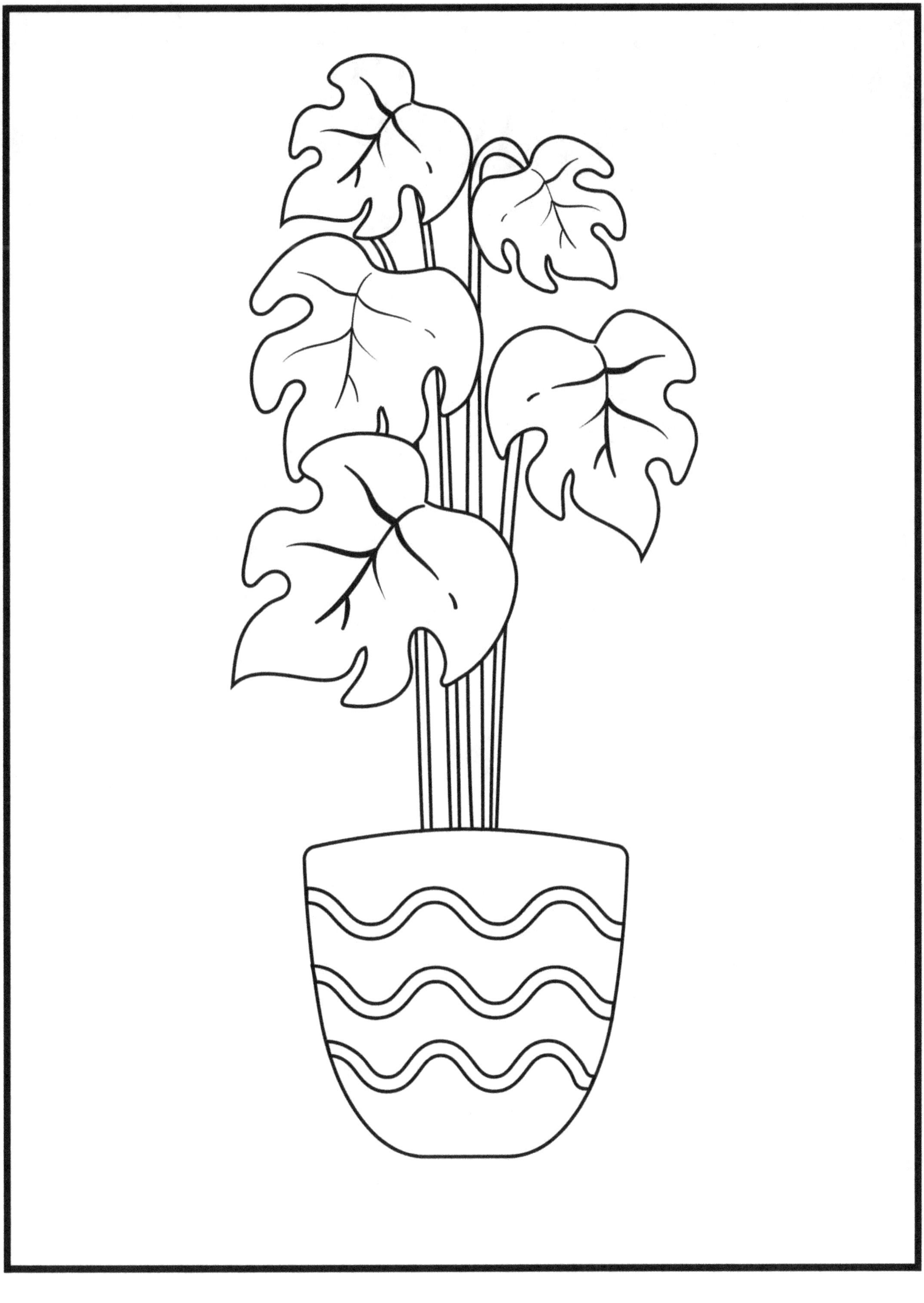

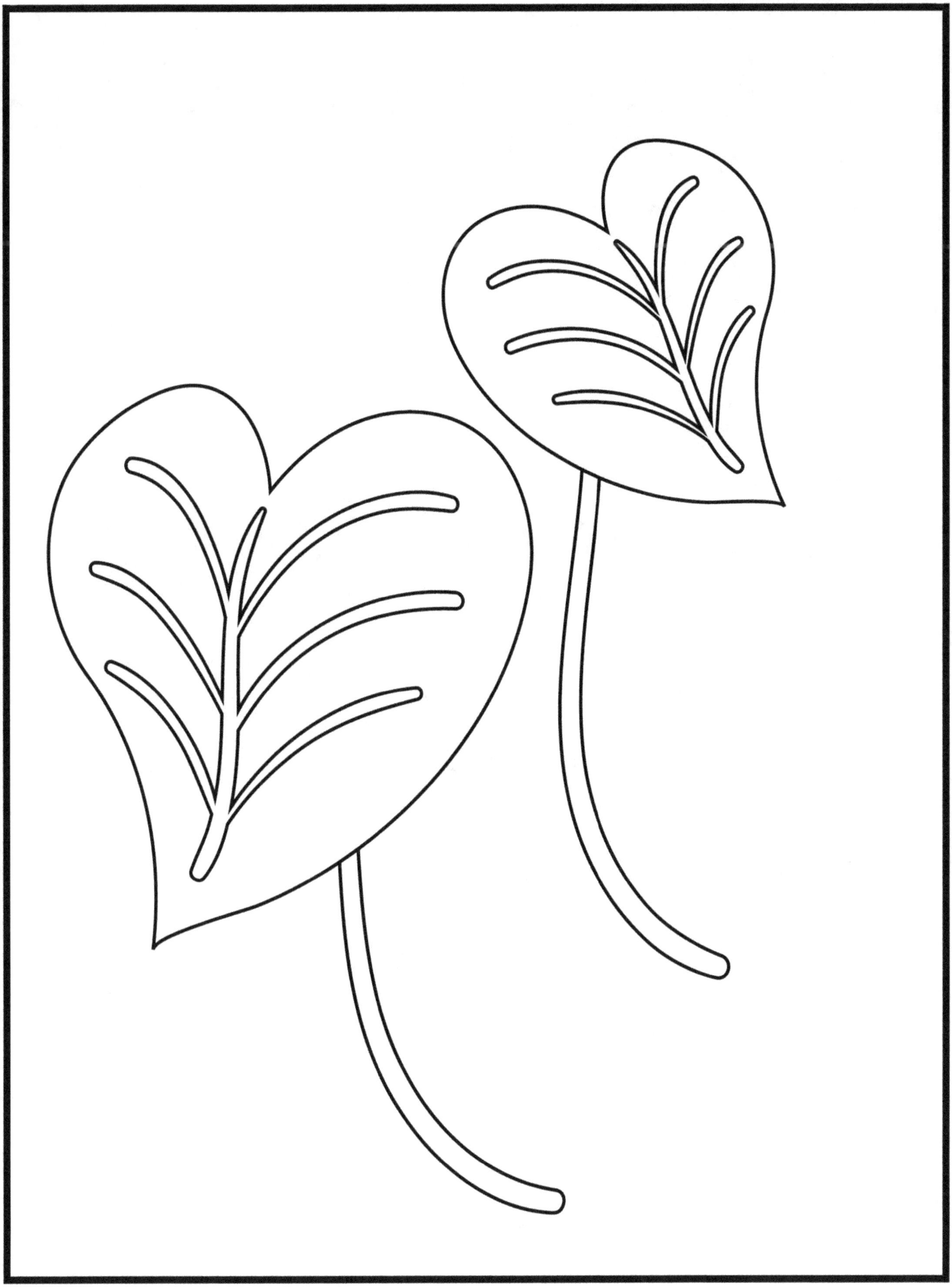

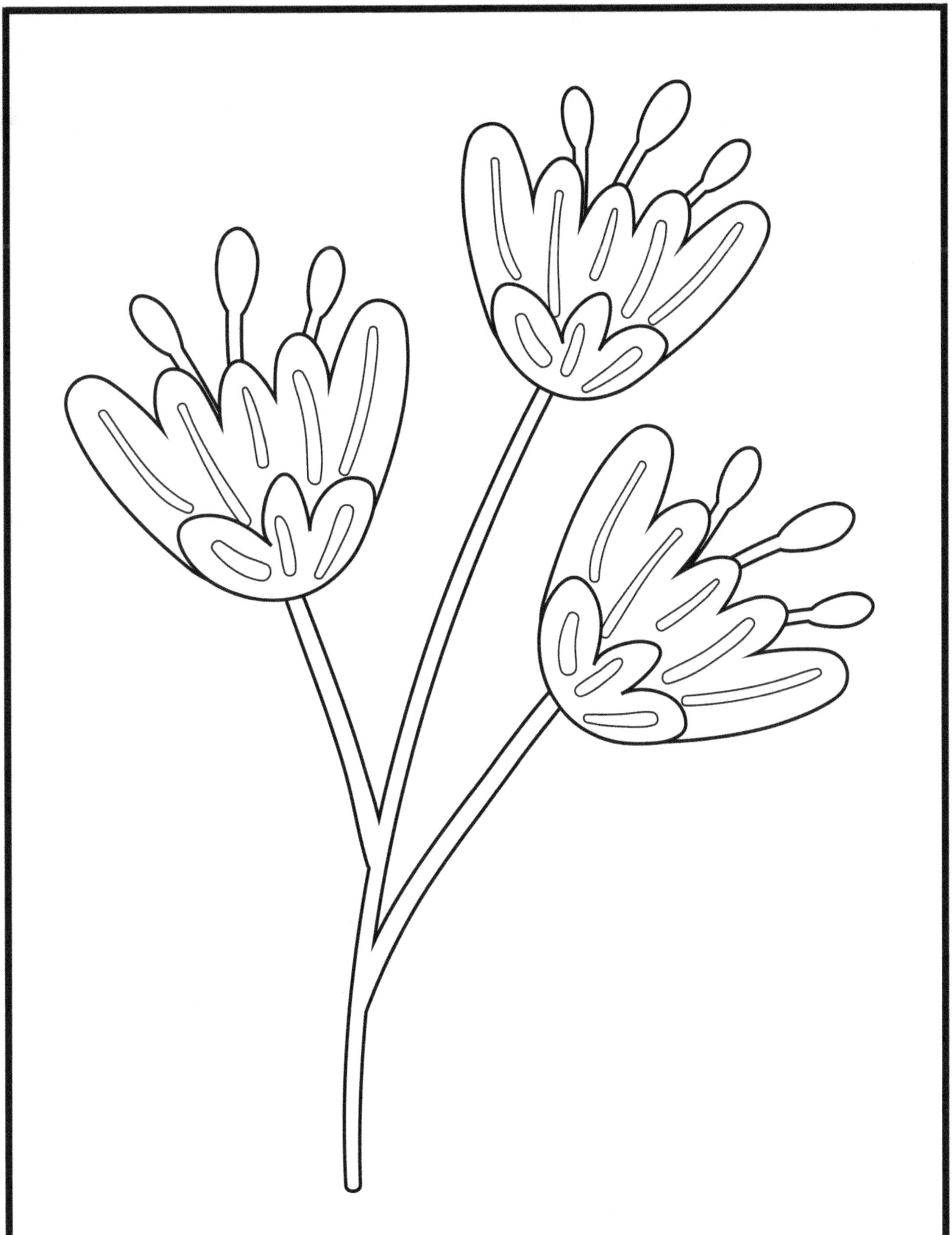

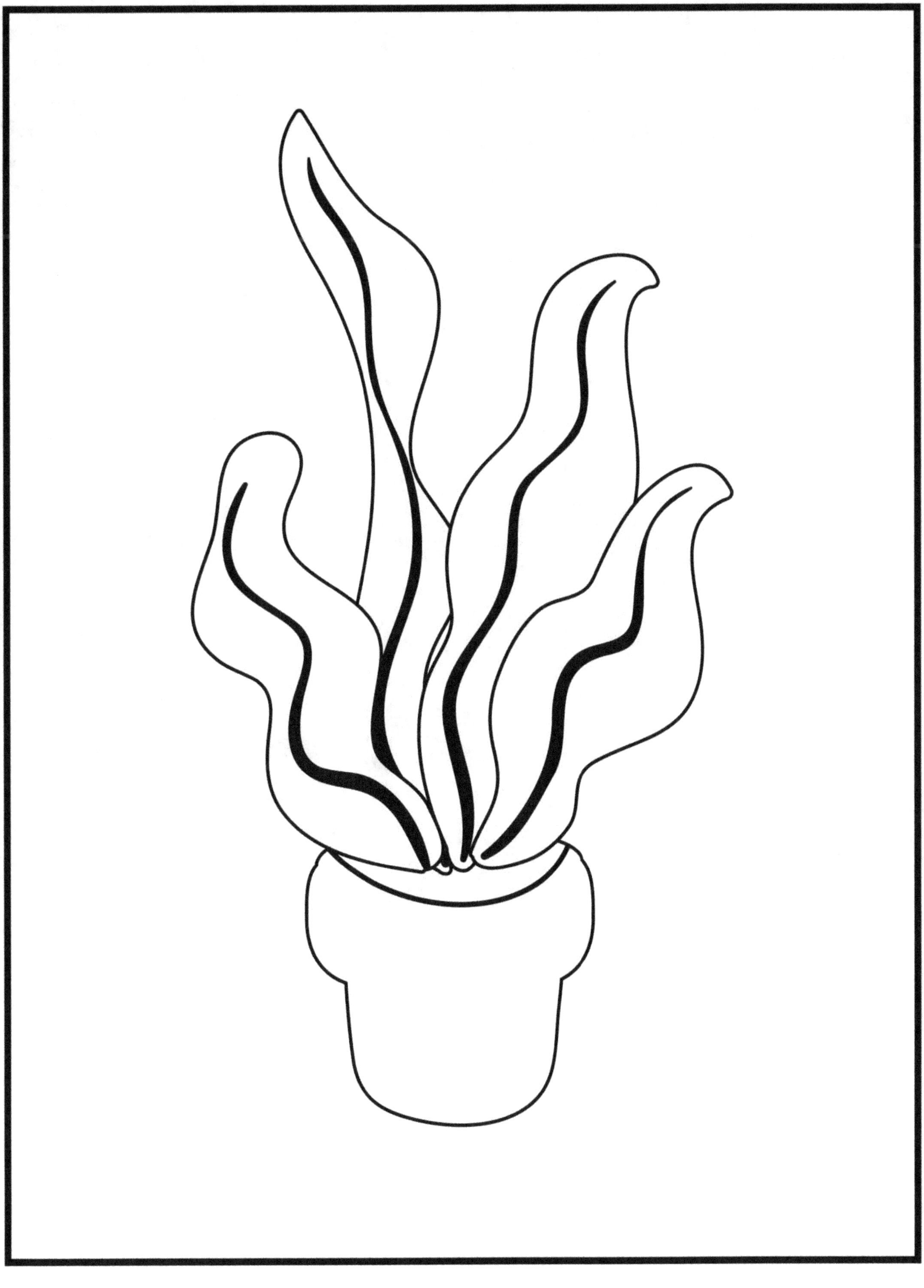

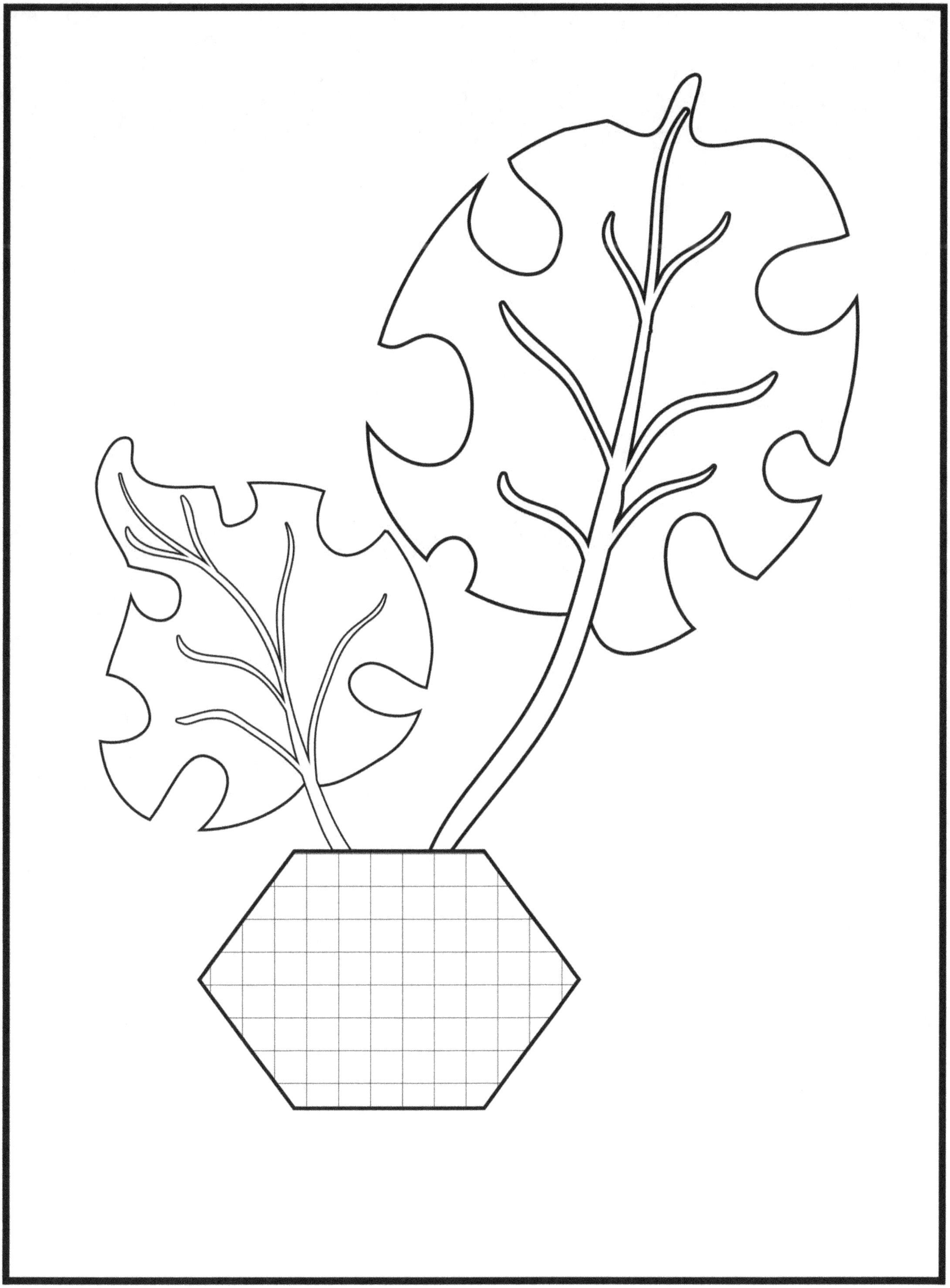

www.ingramcontent.com/pod-product-compliance
Lightning Source LLC
Chambersburg PA
CBHW080622220526
45466CB00010B/3432
9781696793650